Revised & Updated

POP TRIOS for all

Playable on ANY THREE INSTRUMENTS
or any number of instruments in ensemble

Arranged by Michael Story

CONTENTS

Instrumentation

30697	Piano/Conductor/Oboe		30703	Horn in F
30698	Flute/Piccolo		30704	Trombone/Baritone/Bassoon/Tuba
30699	B♭ Clarinet/Bass Clarinet		30705	Violin
30700	Alto Saxophone (E♭ Saxes and E♭ Clarinets)		30706	Viola
30701	Tenor Saxophone		30707	Cello/String Bass
30702	B♭ Trumpet/Baritone T.C.		30708	Percussion

Alfred Music
P.O. Box 10003
Van Nuys, CA 91410-0003
alfred.com

D1088493

ISBN-10: 0-7390-5439-2
ISBN-13: 978-0-7390-5439-0

2

B♭ TRUMPET/BARITONE T.C.

OLD TIME
ROCK AND ROLL

Words and Music by
GEORGE JACKSON and
THOMAS E. JONES III
Arranged by MICHAEL STORY

30702

SING, SING, SING

Words and Music by
LOUIS PRIMA
Arranged by MICHAEL STORY

HEDWIG'S THEME
(From "Harry Potter and the Sorcerer's Stone")

By **JOHN WILLIAMS**
Arranged by MICHAEL STORY

ALL I WANNA DO

Words and Music by
SHERYL CROW, WYN COOPER, KEVIN GILBERT,
BILL BOTTRELL and DAVID BAERWALD
Arranged by MICHAEL STORY

THE MAGNIFICENT SEVEN

By ELMER BERNSTEIN
Arranged by MICHAEL STORY

YOU RAISE ME UP

Words and Music by
ROLF LOVLAND and BRENDAN GRAHAM
Arranged by MICHAEL STORY

30702

MACK THE KNIFE

English Words by MARC BLITZSTEIN
Original German Words by BERT BRECHT

Music by KURT WEILL
Arranged by MICHAEL STORY

*Cue notes indicate optional repeat to measure 3.

THIS IS IT!

Words and Music by
MACK DAVID and JERRY LIVINGSTON
Arranged by MICHAEL STORY

CAN YOU READ MY MIND?

Words by LESLIE BRICUSSE
Music by **JOHN WILLIAMS**
Arranged by MICHAEL STORY

CRAZY IN LOVE

Words and Music by
EUGENE RECORD, RICHARD HARRISON,
BEYONCE KNOWLES, and Sean Carter
Arranged by MICHAEL STORY

15

THE PINK PANTHER

By HENRY MANCINI
Arranged by MICHAEL STORY

Moderate swing feel

STAR WARS
(Main Theme)

By **JOHN WILLIAMS**
Arranged by MICHAEL STORY

I'LL BE THERE FOR YOU
(Theme From "FRIENDS")

Words by DAVID CRANE,
MARTA KAUFFMAN, ALLEE WILLIS,
PHIL SOLEM and DANNY WILDE

Music by MICHAEL SKLOFF
Arranged by MICHAEL STORY

AMERICAN IDIOT

Words by BILLIE JOE
Music by GREEN DAY
Arranged by MICHAEL STORY

HIPS DON'T LIE

Lyrics by SHAKIRA and WYCLEF JEAN
Music by WYCLEF JEAN, JERRY DUPLESSIS, SHAKIRA,
OMAR ALFANNO and LATAVIA PARKER
Arranged by MICHAEL STORY